Because You Are Strong

Because You Are
STRONG

A Study of Godly Strength for Young Men

Daniel Forster

Doorposts

ISBN 978-1-891206-44-3 (print edition)

ISBN 978-1-891206-45-0 (PDF eBook edition)

Doorposts
www.doorposts.com
888-433-4749

This book is dedicated to my son,

Calvin Sterling Forster

May you grow up
to know and love our Lord Jesus,
and may you always find
your strength in Him.

Thank You

To Mama, for letting me take over a project you
started many years ago, and for all your input.

To Katelyn, for helping me make time to write so many times,
and for supporting me so well in this project. I love you.

To Bethany, for taking on more work at Doorposts
so I could get this book finished!

To the young men who "test-drove" these studies
and helped me improve them.

Table of Contents

"I write to you, young men, because you are strong,
and the word of God abides in you,
and you have overcome the evil one."
(1 John 2:14b, ESV)

Introduction

This study was written primarily for young men. Young men have abundant strength and energy, but we don't usually have an over-abundance of wisdom. In order for our strength to be effective, it must be coupled with wisdom from the Word of God. The strength we have is a gift from God, which must be used for His glory. Studying the Scriptures will draw us closer to God. It will also help us wisely exercise and direct every ounce of physical, mental, and spiritual strength He's given to us.

This book will help you accomplish two important things:

The first goal is to *gain a biblical understanding of strength*. God created us with strength, and we need to understand His design for that strength. As young men, we have great strength and potential. We have great abilities that can be used either foolishly, to our destruction, or wisely, for God's glory.

The second goal is to *learn and practice Bible study skills*. This book is designed to give you experience in many different types of Bible study. When you've finished this book, you can take the study methods you've practiced here and continue using them to study any book, chapter, verse, word, person, or topic in the Bible. The ability to study Scripture will serve you well throughout your life, no matter what callings and responsibilities God gives you. If you know God's Word, you'll be prepared to stand strong.

2 Timothy 3:16-17 says "All Scripture is given by inspiration of God, and is profitable for doctrine, for reproof, for correction, for instruction in righteousness: that the man of God may be perfect, thoroughly furnished unto all good works." God's Word tells us how to live and how to please God. We can learn biblical wisdom from pastors and teachers, but we also need to learn through direct, personal interaction with God's Word.

Daily personal Bible reading is important. But we also need to slow down and really *study* God's Word. Personal Bible study brings the Bible to life, and there's no substitute for discovering the depths and riches of God's Word through your own personal study.

It is important, however, that we study what God *actually* says, not what we *think* God says. We need to pray for guidance from the Holy Spirit. In addition, we need to follow sound study practices and use proven resources as we study. Scripture must be interpreted by Scripture, not by other men or the ideas we might read into it. Here are some examples of sound methods you can use while studying the Bible:

- Study original Hebrew or Greek words as they are used throughout Scripture.

- Compare one passage of Scripture with another.

- Observe repeated words and themes in a passage.

- Outline the content of a passage.

- Gather all that Scripture says on a particular topic.

- Study the lives of people in the Bible, noting how their attitudes and actions portray biblical truths.

How this book works:

This book consists of ten studies, with a short review study at the end. Each study is divided into daily assignments which take from five to twenty minutes each. The book contains 74 days worth of study (about 15 weeks if you do five studies a week). You may complete more than one assignment per day if you want to finish faster. Ideas for additional study are given at the end of each study (a total of 40), giving enough direction for up to a whole year of meaningful Bible study.

Using Computers for Bible study:

Digital Bible study tools are becoming more available and affordable, and if you use the Internet, you can find most of the study tools that you'll need for free. These tools can help you study more thoroughly and efficiently. The studies in this book are based on printed study tools, but each study gives optional instructions for using digital Bible study tools (in the gray boxes in the sidebar). Make sure you try the Blue Letter Bible website or app. It's amazing!

Recommended materials:

To fully benefit from these studies, you will need **Nave's Topical Bible** and **Strong's Exhaustive Concordance**. Both books are valuable study tools that you will use over and over again, and they are worth the investment. You can find these books online, at most Christian bookstores, or possibly from your church library. We also offer inexpensive hardbound editions at www.doorposts.com.

Several studies require you to mark words or verses in your Bible, so you will need a Bible that you don't mind marking in and some colored pencils or non-bleeding highlighters.

Bible translations:

The studies in this book use primarily the King James translation of the Bible, because of the many study tools available for this translation. If you prefer to study in a different translation, search for study tools like a concordance and a topical Bible that are designed for your translation. These are becoming increasingly available.

Recommended age levels:

The studies in this book are designed for ages 10-12 and up. Younger boys may be able to complete the studies with help from a parent, older brother, or teacher.

For families with girls:

This study is written primarily for young men, but it's also appropriate for young ladies. Much of what Scripture says about strength applies to women just as much as it does to men. Young ladies can encourage young men towards true, biblical strength. They also need wisdom to discern between true and false strength in their relationships and as they consider marriage. In a few places, alternate questions for young ladies are indicated with "✻". These alternate questions are found in the back of the book.

Strength for the Race

Meditating on Hebrews 11-12

"Wherefore seeing we also are compassed about with so great a cloud of witnesses,
let us lay aside every weight, and the sin which doth so easily beset us,
and let us run with patience the race that is set before us…" (Hebrews 12:1)

This first study will be the simplest form of Bible study: reading a portion of Scripture, meditating on it, and finding application for your life. This is sometimes called the "devotional" method of Bible study. Since meditation and application is a key part of any Bible study, the steps we follow in this first study will serve you well through the rest of this book.

Hebrews 11 contains the "hall of faith," a recounting of faithful deeds by the Old Testament saints, who now make up our "cloud of witnesses." Chapter 12 has specific instructions for us, showing how and why we should imitate Jesus, the One these saints placed their faith in.

These chapters of Hebrews give us *reasons* for being strong along with *examples* of godly men and women who spent their strength in the cause of Christ. From Christian history and from Jesus' example, we can gain the strength to *run with endurance* the race that is set before us, just like these men and women of faith.

Day 1 - Pray and read

A. Pray before you begin reading. You want the Holy Spirit to give you insight and help you see what God is teaching you from His Word as you read.

B. Read chapters 11 and 12 of Hebrews. What are these chapters talking about?

_____

_____

_____

_____

_____

_____

Devotional study:

1. Pray

2. Read the passage of Scripture.

3. Meditate on the passage or selected verses from the passage.

4. Memorize and contemplate verses from the passage.

5. Look at the passage from different angles by asking questions (who, what, where, when, why and how).

6. Pray again and look for specific application to your life.

What you will need:

• Bible

• Colored pencils or highlighters (at least five different colors)

Day 2 - Memorize

A. Our goal is to meditate on this text. Meditating involves **dwelling on** and **contemplating** a passage of Scripture over a period of time. It helps to read it several times. As you read, think about it, and try to understand what it is saying. Something else that can help you meditate on Scripture is to **memorize it**.

B. Memorize key verses from the passage.

Memorize Hebrews 12:1-2. Begin by copying these verses from your Bible into the space below:

Free apps & websites for Bible memory:

*   **Bible Minded**
    (Free Android and Apple app)

*   **Memverse.com**
    (Website with free membership)

*   **Memorize His Word**
    (Free online membership or PC program)

*   **Remember Me**
    (Free Android app, $2.99 for Apple)

*   **Scripture Typer**
    (Free Android & Apple apps.)

*   **Fighter Verses**
    ($2.99 Android and Apple app)

_____

_____

_____

_____

_____

_____

_____

_____

_____

_____

_____

_____

_____

C. Copy these verses a second time on a card or sticky note you can keep with you throughout the day. Read these verses to yourself throughout the day and think about them. Write them out again if it helps you memorize them. Work at this until you can say both verses from memory.

Day 3 - Ask questions

Another aspect of meditation, according to the dictionary, is to "**turn or revolve any subject in the mind**" – to look at it from all sides, so to speak. One way to do this is to **ask questions** of the text you are studying. Any time you are reading the Bible, asking questions (like who, what, why, when, where, and how) will help you understand the text better.

A. Read Hebrews 11-12 again and answer the following questions:

B. Who does this passage hold up as examples for us? As you read, mark each name in chapters 11-12 with the color BROWN. List all the people mentioned by name below:

_____

_____

_____

_____

_____

_____

_____

_____

_____

_____

C. What did these people do? Mark everything that people do in chapter 11 with the color GREEN. List all these actions below:

_____

_____

_____

_____

_____

_____

_____

_____

_____

Meditate:

To **dwell on** any thing in thought; to **contemplate**; to **study**; to **turn or revolve any subject in the mind**; appropriately but not exclusively used of pious contemplation, or a consideration of the great truths of religion.

Webster's 1828 dictionary (emphasis added)

The six questions:

- Who?
- What?
- Why?
- When?
- Where?
- How?

_____

_____

_____

_____

_____

_____

D. Why did they do these things? **How** did they remain strong in these trials? You've probably noticed a key word that occurs repeatedly in chapter 11.

This word is _____.

Mark every instance of this word with BLUE.

Day 4 - More questions

A. When did the events in Hebrews 11 take place?

_____

_____

B. What does Jesus do? Read Hebrews 12:1-4 and mark everything Jesus does with the color RED. List these actions below:

_____

_____

_____

_____

_____

_____

C. What are we encouraged to do? Read chapter 12 and mark anything this chapter says we should **do** with the color GREEN. List everything you mark here:

_____

_____

_____

_____

_____

_____

_____

_____

_____

_____

_____

_____

_____

_____

D. Why should we do these things? Mark any reasons given in chapter 12 with the color ORANGE and list them here:

_____

_____

_____

_____

_____

_____

_____

_____

_____

_____

_____

Bible programs, sites, and mobile apps:

- **BlueLetterBible.org**
  (Website and free apps) The best Bible study website. Easily search for words and verses, compare translations, check cross-references, study words, read commentaries, listen to audio and more. It's all free too!

- **BibleGateway.com**
  (Website and free apps) Good for Bible reading. Contains the most Bible translations and languages, but has few study helps. Apps require wifi/data connection even to read Bibles.

- **E-sword.net**
  (Free PC and Mac install, inexpensive iPad and iPhone apps) Has many study tools, including concordance, topical Bible, and commentaries.

- **BibleStudyTools.com**
  (Website only) A quick way to use study tools like the concordance, topical Bible, and commentaries, all for free.

- **Bible.is**
  (Website and free apps) Study functions are limited, but this site lets you listen online or download audio for any Bible passage.

- **Apple & Android Apps**
  Find free ESV and KJV Bible apps in the app stores.

- **Amazon Kindle**
  Free ESV, KJV, and NIV Bibles are available on Kindle readers and any computer or device that runs the free Kindle app.

Day 5 - Review and application

Now you're ready to consider a **personal application of this text for your own life**. Pray again for God's guidance!

A. Review the notes you made when answering the questions. From the godly examples in Hebrews 11, what did you notice? How can you be more like these men of faith?

_____

_____

_____

_____

_____

_____

_____

_____

_____

_____

_____

_____

_____

_____

B. Several specific instructions were given in Hebrews 12. Can you see any areas where God is calling you to change?

_____

_____

_____

_____

_____

_____

_____

_____

_____

Application

It's important that your application is both **specific** and **achievable**. A thought or feeling isn't true application unless you take action or make a noticeable change in your life. "I want to be more diligent" is a good goal, but if you make the specific goal, "I will get up at 6:30 and do my chores every day this week" you are more likely to grow in diligence.

_____

_____

_____

_____

_____

_____

_____

_____

_____

C. Decide on 2-3 specific things you will do to live out the application you have discovered from Hebrews 11-12, and write them below.

_____

_____

_____

_____

_____

_____

_____

_____

_____

_____

_____

_____

_____

For further study:

- Conduct a topical study on perseverance. Look up "Perseverance" in **Nave's Topical Bible**, read the verses in this section, and take notes. Who persevered in the Bible? Why should we persevere? What are some of the blessings of perseverance?

- Conduct a topical study on "faith," using either a topical Bible (see Study 2) or a concordance (see Study 3).

- Conduct a character study focused on one of the men mentioned in Hebrews 11. Follow the character study method used in Study 4.

- Study Hebrews 12:1 using the method outlined in Study 6.

Study 2

Strength with No Limits

A Topical Study on the Omnipotence of God

"O LORD God of hosts, who is a strong LORD like unto thee?" (Psalm 89:8a)

This study focuses on one of God's many attributes: His omnipotence. This is our first **topical study,** and we'll learn to use **Nave's Topical Bible** to find verses on this topic. The tools we use in this study and the next may be used to study any topic in the Bible.

In theological writings, God's omnipotence is usually categorized under His "incommunicable" attributes (those that men do not share with Him). However, some theologians count God's omnipotence with the "communicable" attributes, making the case that God does share this part of His character with us, only in a limited way. Even though we aren't all-powerful like God, He does share His power with us to a degree. Any strength we have is a gift from Him, and He alone gives us the ability to accomplish things in the world (only our strength is limited, while His is infinite).

Pure and ultimate strength is found only in God, so we should look to Him to understand what true strength looks like. Understanding God's all-powerfulness should increase our trust in Him and give us a better perspective on the limited strength of men. It also reminds us that, as followers of Christ, God's unstoppable power is at work in us and through us.

Day 1 - Find verses using Nave's Topical Bible

Topics are arranged alphabetically by topic in Nave's. A wide variety of theological and practical topics are covered. In the complete edition, the full text of verses on frequently used subjects are fully quoted, while less-common topics list only the references.

A. Look up "GOD – OMNIPOTENT" in Nave's Topical Bible. You will find about 9 verses listed. Record the references below, leaving room to record your observations.

Reference: Observations:

_____

_____

_____

_____

Topical study:

1. Find verses on your topic using a topical Bible and/or concordance.

2. Read verses and record your observations.

3. Summarize your findings.

4. Application

What you will need:

- Your Bible

- Nave's Topical Bible

Omnipotence:

1 Almighty power; unlimited or infinite power; a word in strictness applicable only to God. Hence it is sometimes used for God. The works of creation demonstrate the omnipotence of God.

2. Unlimited power over particular things; as the omnipotence of love.

(Webster's 1828 Dictionary)

Nave's Topical Bible search online:

1. Go to www.biblestudytools.com.

1. Go to the "Study" tab and click "Concordances" in the drop-down box.

2. In this list, find "Nave's Topical Bible" and click on it.

3. Scroll down and you'll see links for each letter of the alphabet. Click the "G" and find "God".

4. The "God" section is several pages long, so you might have to click the "Continued" link at the bottom to get to "GOD-Omnipotent". Nine reference links are given in this section.

5. If you Ctrl+click these links on a PC, they will open in a new tab where you can read each one.

Reference: Observations:

_____

_____

_____

_____

_____

_____

_____

_____

_____

B. Look up each of these references and read them, along with the verses that precede and follow them. Knowing the context may help you understand some of the verses better. Record your observations in the space above for each verse.

Day 2 - Additional topics in Nave's

A. After the verses listed in the "GOD – Omnipotent" section of Nave's, you will see some additional notes. The first one says:

"For uses of the term Almighty consult Concordances."

This means that you can find additional Scripture references related to this topic by looking up the word "Almighty" in a concordance. We won't look these up, because we'll find many of the same verses in just a minute using **Nave's**. We will start using a concordance in the next study.

B. The final note says:

"See Creator, above; Power of, Preserver, below."

This refers to other related topics in Nave's. Let's look these up.

Look up the section "GOD – Creator." You will find several pages of verses all related to God as the creator of the world. We will not study these in detail right now, but you can keep in mind that God's power is demonstrated through His creating of the world.

Look up the section "GOD – Preserver" You will see that it also contains several pages of verses. We will also skip these for this study, but you may want to read them at another time.

Look up the section "GOD – POWER OF" This section also gives several pages of Bible verses related to God's power. This topic is the most relevant since we're studying God's omnipotence, so we'll look at these verses more carefully.

C. Verses on the power of God. Since there are so many verses, we will not look each one up in the Bible, but Nave's (if you're using the print edition) should give the full text of each verse. Read all the verses in this section of Nave's and note your observations below.

_____

_____

_____

_____

_____

_____

_____

_____

_____

_____

_____

_____

_____

_____

_____

_____

_____

_____

_____

_____

_____

_____

Nave's Topical Bible

This Bible study tool was created over 100 years ago by a US Army chaplain, Orville J. Nave. He studied the King James Bible and labored for 14 years, along with his wife Anna, his "indefatigable assistant," to create the best-known topical Bible we have today. Earlier topical Bibles only covered a few topics and wouldn't include a passage in more than one category, even if it was relevant to multiple topics. Nave's Topical Bible contains more than 100,000 Bible verses organized under 20,000 different topics. This study tool is much more complete, and therefore more useful to everyone.

"Its preparation was inspired by the obvious deficiency of such helps in the use of the Scriptures. This deficiency was felt by the author in preparing sermons, lectures, and other forms of religious instruction. The quiet of army garrisons, apart from the rush and distraction of dense communities, has been favorable to its careful preparation. With the belief that it will contribute to make the Scriptures more quickly, easily, and fully available where particular subjects are under consideration, I offer it to the public." – Orville Nave

Day 3 - Summarize

Review your notes above, and organize your observations under the following topics:

A. The extent of God's power:

_____

_____

_____

_____

_____

_____

_____

B. Comparing God to others:

_____

_____

_____

_____

_____

_____

_____

_____

_____

_____

C. How God uses His power:

_____

_____

_____

_____

_____

Attributes of God
• Knowledge
• Wisdom
• Supremacy
• Sovereignty
• Immutability
• Omnipotence
• Omnipresence
• Holiness
• Faithfulness
• Goodness
• Patience
• Mercy
• Love
• Wrath
• Justice

_____

_____

_____

_____

_____

_____

_____

_____

D. God's strength is never-ending:

_____

_____

_____

_____

_____

_____

_____

E. Ways we can imitate God's use of power:

_____

_____

_____

_____

_____

_____

_____

_____

_____

_____

_____

_____

F. Summarize God's omnipotence in your own words. Considering what you have learned from Scripture, what does it mean to say God is "omnipotent?"

_____

_____

_____

_____

_____

_____

_____

_____

_____

_____

_____

_____

_____

_____

_____

_____

_____

Day 4 - Application

A. Think now about what you can apply in your own life. Pray that God will show you how you can be more like Him.

B. Do these observations give you a better idea of what godly strength looks like?

_____

_____

C. What about God's strength stands out to you most in this study?

_____

_____

_____

D. Does understanding God's omnipotence give you courage or comfort in any way?

_____

_____

_____

_____

E. How is God calling you to be more like Him?

_____

_____

_____

_____

_____

_____

_____

_____

_____

For additional study:

- Look up "Jesus, the Christ" in Nave's Topical Bible, and read the verses under the heading, "Jesus, the Christ. – Omnipotence of". Note anything else you learn about God's omnipotence as expressed through Jesus.

- The word "Omnipotent" is used once in the KJV Bible. The Greek word in this instance is translated "Almighty" in other instances. Conduct a word study on the word "Almighty" in the Old and New Testaments using the directions from Study 5.

- Read the verses listed under "GOD – Creator" and "GOD – Preserver" in Nave's Topical Bible.

- Choose another attribute of God (see p. 15) and study it using the same methods you used in this study.

F. Write down one specific thing you will do to apply what you learned in this study:

_____

_____

_____

_____

_____

_____

_____

_____

_____

Strength and Wisdom

A Topical Study in Proverbs

"A wise man is strong; yea, a man of knowledge increaseth strength." (Proverbs 24:5)

This is our second topical study. We'll refer to **Nave's Topical Bible** again, but since this topic is not covered well in Nave's, we'll use another study tool, **Strong's Concordance**. This is a study tool that helps you find specific words wherever they are used in the Bible.

This is a topical study on "strength," but we'll narrow our study to one book of the Bible, to keep the study manageable. You might be surprised at how much we will find in just one book! The book of Proverbs was written first and foremost for young men, and Solomon's wisdom will help us discern between true strength and false strength.

Day 1 - Word definitions, topical Bible

A. Look up the word "strength" in an English dictionary, and write the definition:

_____

_____

_____

B. Look up strength in a thesaurus (or at www.thesaurus.com). List any synonyms for the word "strength":

_____

_____

_____

C. List some antonyms (opposites) of strength:

_____

_____

_____

_____

Topical study:

1. Find verses on your topic using a topical Bible and/or concordance.

2. Read verses and record your observations.

3. Summarize findings.

4. Application

What you will need:

- Nave's Topical Bible

- Strong's Exhaustive Concordance

- An English dictionary

- Synonym finder/thesaurus

Strong's Concordance

Strong's Exhaustive Concordance was compiled by James Strong, a Methodist Bible scholar in the late 1800's. Dr. Strong was not a pastor, but he served as Professor of Exegetical Theology at Drew Theological Seminary (now Drew University) in Madison, New Jersey. He was one of five men who formed the core faculty of this seminary from its inception in 1867. He traveled in Europe, Israel, and Egypt while doing research for another theological work. He served as mayor of his hometown and built his own railroad company. He was known for his pursuit of excellence, and he was an enthusiastic and respected teacher. A Dr. Buckley said of him,

"At night in his library, he worked like a plow-horse, but in the lecture room he was as frisky as a colt. No one ever went to sleep in his classes unless he was out of health or an imbecile."

Dr. Strong could see the value that an exhaustive concordance would be to Bible scholars, in a day when no such reference tool existed. He worked for thirty-five years to catalog and organize every single word used in the King James version of the Bible into a complete concordance, assigning numbers to the original Hebrew and Greek words and creating a dictionary of these words as well. The work was finally published in 1890, just four years before he died. Today, computers make this job much easier, but he did all the work by hand.

D. Now we will begin to look for verses in the book of Proverbs.

In our last topical study, we found most of our verses by looking up the topic in Nave's Topical Bible. This is always a good way to begin a topical study. Look up "strength" in Nave's.

Are there any verses from Proverbs? _____

E. Does it list any other related topics? Look up any related topics, and look for verses from Proverbs.

Do you see any verses from Proverbs? _____

For this topic, Nave's is not very helpful, so we'll move on to the next step.

Day 2 - How to read a concordance listing

A **concordance** is a study tool that helps you look up specific words in the Bible. Your Bible may have a concordance in the back, and it will list some of the verses we're looking for, but the list is not complete. For this study (and others in this book), we will use **Strong's Exhaustive Concordance**, which covers **every word** used in the Bible. If you are serious about Bible study, this reference book is an important addition to your library.

A. Look up a word in Strong's Concordance

Words are listed alphabetically in a concordance. Look up the word "strength" (Note: Strong's Exhaustive Concordance is based on the King James Version of the Bible.)

You'll see something like this:

```
STRENGTH
Gen   4:12 yield unto thee her s; a fugitive and a        H3581
      49: 3 the beginning of my s, the excellency of      H202
         24 But his bow abode in s, and the arms of       H386
Ex   13: 3 of bondage; for by s of hand the LORD          H2392
         14 say unto him, By s of hand the LORD           H2392
         16 thine eyes: for by s of hand the LORD         H2392
      14:27 sea returned to his s when the morning        H386
      15: 2 The LORD is my s and song, and he is          H5797
         13 them in thy s unto thy holy habitation.       H5797
Lev  26:20 And your s shall be spent in vain: for         H3581
Nu   23:22 he hath as it were the s of an unicorn.        H8443
      24: 8 hath as it were the s of an unicorn: he       H8443
```

The abbreviations and numbers at the **beginning of each line** indicate the reference of each verse in which the word *strength* is used. (If you're unfamiliar with standard abbreviations for the books of the Bible, refer to the list provided at the beginning of the concordance. You may want to copy this list and keep it as a marker in your concordance while you are studying.)

The words in the **center of each line** quote the portion of each verse that contains the word **strength**. Each bold "**s**" indicates where the word *strength* is used in that verse.

The numbers on the **right side** correspond to the original Hebrew or Greek word that was translated *strength* in your Bible. We'll look up original words using these numbers in the dictionary part of Strong's later, in Study 5.

B. Look for references that come from the book of Proverbs.

Skim the section on **strength** until you find references from the book of Proverbs. Write down these references below (one per line, leaving room to summarize each one later):

Reference: Notes:

_____

_____

_____

_____

_____

_____

_____

C. Now look for the word "strong" in your concordance and write down any references from Proverbs:

Reference: Notes:

_____

_____

_____

_____

_____

_____

_____

Look up a word in Strong's Concordance online

1. Go to www.biblestudytools.com.

2. Click on "Study" in the upper tool bar.

3. Click on "Concordances".

4. Click on "Strong's Exhaustive Concordance".

5. Type in "strength" in the "Search the Bible with Strong's" box and click "Search".

6. This search generates 232 results, but you can filter the results and show only those from the book of Proverbs.

Word search with Blue Letter Bible

1. Go to www.blueletterbible.org.

2. Type "strong" in the search box and hit enter.

3. You will get a list of all verses in the Bible that use the word "strong".

4. You can narrow these results to just the Old or New Testament, or to a specific book of the Bible.

5. Each verse has a button to access "tools" and study deeper (in the app, just tap on the verse you want to study).

_____

_____

_____

_____

Now we will look up some synonyms for "strength".

D. Look up the word "power" in your concordance and record any references from Proverbs:

Reference: Notes:

_____

_____

E. Look up the word "mighty," and record any references from Proverbs:

Reference: Notes:

_____

_____

_____

_____

F. If you thought of any other words synonymous with "strength," look them up in Strong's and record any Proverbs references you find:

Reference: Notes:

_____

_____

_____

_____

G. The main antonym of "strength" is the word "weak". This is relevant to our topical study, so look up the words "weak" and "weakness" in Strong's. You'll see that these words are not used in Proverbs at all.

Day 3 - Read verses in Proverbs

A. Now, take your Bible and look up each of the references you recorded above. Beside each reference you just copied, summarize what the verse says about strength.

Day 4 - Summarize your findings

After you have read and summarized each verse, review your notes. Do you see any common or repeated themes? Organize your notes under the following topics:

A. Who is strong or mighty in Proverbs?

_____

_____

_____

_____

_____

_____

_____

_____

_____

_____

B. Where do men often look for strength?

_____

_____

_____

_____

_____

C. Where do we find true strength?

_____

_____

_____

_____

_____

_____

_____

D. What good is strength?

_____

_____

_____

_____

_____

_____

E. What is better than strength?

_____

_____

_____

_____

_____

F. What things can overcome strength?

_____

_____

_____

_____

_____

_____

G. What effect does the strange woman have on strong men in Proverbs 7:26 and 31:3?

_____

_____

_____

_____

_____

_____

H. Read Proverbs 31:10-31. In what ways does a virtuous woman use her strength?

_____

_____

_____

_____

_____

_____

I. In your own words, summarize what Proverbs teaches about strength:

_____

_____

_____

_____

_____

_____

_____

_____

_____

_____

_____

Day 5 - Application

A. ✱ Based on what you have just learned, what can you do to be a stronger man or to use your strength more wisely? Is there a specific area where God is calling you to exercise your strength or to grow stronger in?

_____

_____

_____

_____

_____

_____

_____

_____

_____

• Conduct a similar topical study on strength in another book of the Bible (try Psalms or Isaiah).

• Study Proverbs 24:10-12 using the verse study method from Study 6.

• Proverbs 16:32 says "He that is slow to anger is better than the mighty; and he that ruleth his spirit than he that taketh a city." Look up the following verses and note what you learn about being "slow to anger" and "ruling the spirit" (Prov. 14:29, 15:18, Eccl. 7:8).

• We learned in this study that strength must be paired with wisdom. Using the same methods you used in this study, conduct another topical study on "wisdom" in the book of Proverbs.

B. How can you grow stronger in this area? List at least two specific things that you will do. Give yourself a specific goal and time frame:

_____

_____

_____

_____

_____

_____

_____

_____

_____

Strength and Temptation

A Character Study of Samson

"And the woman bore a son and called his name Samson. And the young man grew, and the LORD blessed him." (Judges 13:24)

Samson is probably the strongest man who ever lived, physically speaking. God gave him extreme strength, which he used to protect and deliver God's people. Samson is commended for his faith, but he also showed weakness when he was tempted, and we can learn much from his story.

The focus of a character study is to learn all we can about a specific Bible character. We'll use study tools like the concordance and Bible dictionary to find every reference to Samson in the Bible.

Day 1 - Read Samson's story in the Bible

A. Find the story of Samson in the Bible (Search for "Samson" in a concordance or Bible app if you need help). Write down the book and chapters that contain his story, and any other references to Samson in the Bible:

_____

_____

_____

_____

_____

_____

B. Read these chapters, and any other references, observing what is said about Samson.

Day 2 -Researching Samson

Review the passages you read yesterday and answer the questions below:

A. Meaning of his name: (look up in a Bible dictionary or encyclopedia)

_____

_____

Character study:

1. Find and read his story in the Bible.

2. Look up background information using study helps.

3. Look for themes and connections with other parts of Scripture.

4. Write a biographical sketch.

5. Seek to answer any questions you have.

6. Find application for your own life.

What you will need:

- Your Bible

- Concordance

- Bible dictionary or encyclopedia

- Bible atlas (or use Bible maps online)

Bible word search online:

1. Go to www.blueletterbible.org, www.biblestudytools.com or www.biblegateway.com.

2. Find the prominent "search" box, type "Samson," and hit enter.

3. You should see a list of all Bible references that mention Samson.

Look up Samson in a Bible dictionary online

1. Go to www.blueletterbible.org.

2. Click on "STUDY" in the upper tool bar.

3. Under "BIBLE REFERENCE," click on "Encyclopedias/Dictionaries".

4. Select "S" and then "Sa-" and scroll down to find "Samson."

5. You'll find info from several Bible dictionaries explaining the meaning of his name, where he is mentioned in Scripture, etc.

B. His family and ancestry:

_____

_____

_____

C. Places he lived and traveled: (List the names of places, then look these up in a Bible atlas, Bible encyclopedia or online maps.)

_____

_____

_____

_____

D. The times in which he lived: (Read Judges 2:16-23, 21:25)

_____

_____

_____

E. The main events of his life:

_____

_____

_____

_____

_____

_____

_____

_____

_____

_____

_____

F. Note every time the "Spirit of the Lord" is mentioned in Judges 13-16:

_____

_____

_____

_____

_____

_____

_____

_____

Finding Bible maps online

- At www.biblemap.org, you can enter book and chapter of the Bible that you are reading, and it will pinpoint any locations on the map for you.

- At www.biblestudy.org/maps, scroll down and find the map of "Palestine in the time of Israel's Judges".

- At www.bible.ca/maps/, scroll down the page and you will find a map that covers the time of Samson.

Day 3 - Additional details

Review Judges 14-16 and look for additional details about Samson's life:

A. His acts of obedience: (How did he show strength of character? How did he serve others?)

_____

_____

_____

_____

_____

_____

_____

B. His acts of physical strength: (Who did he protect? Who did he harm? What did he accomplish?)

_____

_____

_____

_____

_____

_____

_____

_____

_____

_____

C. Temptations he faced:

_____

_____

_____

_____

_____

_____

_____

_____

_____

D. His shortcomings and apparent mistakes: (When did he fail to exercise self-control? How did he lose his strength?)

_____

_____

_____

_____

_____

_____

_____

_____

E. Compare Judges 14:15-18 and Judges 16:4-20. Read Proverbs 26:11. What does Proverbs call someone who does the same foolish thing over and over again?

_____

_____

F. ✻ Samson had several relationships with Philistine women, against the advice of his parents. Twice, he was deceived by these women and these relationships turned out to be his downfall. What could Samson have done differently to avoid being deceived by these women?

Genesis 39:7-12

Deuteronomy 7:1-4

Proverbs 5:1-8

Proverbs 6:20-26

Proverbs 7:24-27

Day 4 - Additional background info

A. Read Numbers 6. What do you learn about Nazirites?

_____

B. How does this help you understand Samson better?

_____

_____

_____

C. Read Hebrews 11. What do you learn about Samson from this passage?

_____

_____

_____

_____

D. Several other men in the Bible were born to barren women. Can you name them?

_____

_____

_____

E. Read the following verses. What is similar to Samson's story?

Genesis 17:15-21

_____

_____

Genesis 25:21-23

_____

_____

Genesis 29:31, 30:22

_____

_____

1 Samuel 1:1-2:26

_____

_____

Luke 1:5-2:40

_____

_____

_____

_____

_____

_____

_____

_____

_____

_____

Day 5 - Biographical sketch

A. Review your notes and write a short biographical sketch of Samson:

_____

_____

_____

_____

_____

_____

_____

_____

_____

_____

_____

_____

_____

_____

_____

B. Note any questions you have about the life of Samson. List any events in this story that you do not understand or Scripture passages that are unclear to you.

_____

_____

_____

_____

C. Seek to answer these questions by asking your parents, asking your pastor, or by consulting a Bible dictionary or commentary (i.e. Matthew Henry's commentary, see more info on p. 62).

_____

_____

_____

_____

_____

Day 6 - Summary and application

A. List several descriptive words that describe Samson's character:

_____

_____

_____

B. What lessons can you learn from Samson's life?

_____

_____

_____

_____

_____

_____

_____

_____

C. In what areas is God calling you to change after studying Samson's life?

_____

_____

_____

_____

_____

_____

_____

_____

_____

_____

For additional study:

• Using the same methods from this study, conduct a character study on Gideon, another Spirit-empowered judge of Israel.

• Samson was not the only strong man that stumbled because of his lust. Study 2 Samuel 11 and 12 using the chapter study method from Study 7. Note how David was tempted, how he failed, and also how he showed godly repentance.

• Conduct a topical study on Spirit-empowered men. Begin by looking up "Holy Spirit – Inspiration of" in Nave's topical Bible.

Strength to be Valiant

A Word Study on "Valor"

"And the angel of the LORD appeared unto him, and said unto him, The LORD is with thee, thou mighty man of valour." (Judges 6:12)

In this study, we will study the word "valor" and the "valiant" men of the Bible. "Valor" is possibly the highest form of human strength we see in the Bible. The Hebrew word for "valor" is translated many different ways, and by tracking down and noting these other uses, we'll understand better what the word means and how we can be "valiant" men.

You learned how to look up a word in Strong's Concordance in Study 3, and we'll do that again in this study. This time we'll use the Hebrew dictionary section of Strong's to find the definition of the word, along with other ways the original Hebrew word was used and how it's translated in your Bible.

Day 1 - Find the English definition of your word

A. Look up "valor" in an English dictionary (in print or online). If you're using an older dictionary like Webster's 1828, it will be spelled "valour" like it is in the King James Bible. Copy the definition of "valor" here:

_____

_____

_____

_____

_____

B. Look for the adjective form, "valiant," and record it's definition too:

_____

_____

_____

_____

_____

Word study:

1. Look up the English definition.

2. Look up the word in a concordance, read verses that use that word.

3. Find the Strong's number and look up the original word and definition.

4. Look up verses where the word is translated differently and read them.

5. Summarize your findings.

6. Application

What you will need:

- Strong's Exhaustive Concordance

- An English dictionary

- A notebook

Look up original Hebrew or Greek words with Blue Letter Bible

1. Go to www.blueletterbible.org.

2. Search for the word "valour". You will get a list of 37 verses that use this word in the KJV.

3. The first verse to use this word is Joshua 1:14. Use the "tools" button on the left (or tap the verse itself in the BLB app). Select the "interlinear" option.

4. Each phrase of the verse is displayed with the corresponding Hebrew word beside it. Scroll down to the phrase "men of valor".

5. You will see the phrase, followed by "H2428", then the word as it is written and pronounced in Hebrew ("chayil").

6. Click on "H2428" and you open a gold mine of information about this word!

7. Under "Root Word (Etymology)" you will see the root word that chayil is based on.

8. Under "KJV Translation Count" you will see all the different English words that are used in place of this word in the KJV Bible, and how many times each word is used.

9. The next sections give you definitions of the word and insights into its meaning as used in Scripture.

10. To get an even better understanding of the word as it is used throughout the Old Testament, you can skim the bottom section under "Concordance Results Using KJV" and read every other verse that uses this same Hebrew word.

C. Look up the word *valour* in Strong's Concordance (Note: Strong's is based on the **King James Version** of the Bible. If you're using a concordance designed for a different Bible translation, look for the modern spelling, ***valor***.)

You'll find a list of references and excerpts from verses. Each bold "**v**" indicates where the word ***valour*** is used in that verse.

VALOUR

Jos	1:14	all the mighty men of **v**, and help them;	H2428
	6: 2	king thereof, *and* the mighty men of **v**.	H2428
	8: 3	men of **v**, and sent them away by night.	H2428
	10: 7	with him, and all the mighty men of **v**.	H2428
Jdg	3:29	men of **v**; and there escaped not a man.	H2428
	6:12	*is* with thee, thou mighty man of **v**.	H2428
	11: 1	a mighty man of **v**, and he *was* the son	H2428
	18: 2	coasts, men of **v**, from Zorah, and from	H2428
	20:44	thousand men; all these *were* men of **v**.	H2428
	46	drew the sword; all these *were* men of **v**.	H2428
1Ki	11:28	a mighty man of **v**: and Solomon seeing	H2428
2Ki	5: 1	a mighty man in **v**, *but he was* a leper.	H2428

The words in the center of each line quote the portion of each verse that contains the word ***valour***.

D. Dictionary numbers. The words listed **at the end of each line** are numbers that correspond to the definition numbers at the back of **Strong's Exhaustive Concordance**. Notice that all the words listed under valour have the **same number** following them. This means that the same original Hebrew word was used in all of these verses.

What number has the concordance assigned to this word? _____

E. Hebrew or Greek? Numbers for references from the **Old Testament** are listed in standard type (and may be preceded by an "H") and indicate that these words will be listed in the **Hebrew** portion of the dictionary. This dictionary appears **first** at the back of **Strong's**.

Numbers for **New Testament** references appear in *italic type* (and may be preceded by a "G"). These definitions will appear in the **Greek** dictionary, which follows the Hebrew one.

All **Old Testament words** will be defined in the **Hebrew dictionary**; all **New Testament words** will be defined in the **Greek dictionary**. The difference in type style for their numbers will help you remember this.

Which dictionary will you use to look up the definition for number 2428?

Day 2 - How to read a dictionary entry:

Look up number 2428 in the Hebrew dictionary of Strong's.

A. Following the number is the **original word** as it is written in Hebrew.

❑ Circle or highlight this word:

> **H2428** חַיִל *hayil* from H2342; probably a *force,* whether of men, means or other resources; an *army, wealth, virtue, valor, strength:*— able, activity, army, army, band of men, band of soldiers, company, forces, great forces, goods, host, might, power, riches, strength, strong, substance, train, valiant, valiant, valiantly, valour, virtuous, virtuously, war, worthy, worthily.

B. Next follows the precise **pronunciation** of the Hebrew word, spelled out in English letters.

❑ Circle or highlight this pronunciation:

> **H2428** חַיִל *hayil* from H2342; probably a *force,* whether of men, means or other resources; an *army, wealth, virtue, valor, strength:*— able, activity, army, army, band of men, band of soldiers, company, forces, great forces, goods, host, might, power, riches, strength, strong, substance, train, valiant, valiant, valiantly, valour, virtuous, virtuously, war, worthy, worthily.

C. After pronunciation, the **etymology** of the word is given. This is the history of the word, tracing it back to its root word or words. In this case, ***hayil*** comes from the root word 2342 ***chul*** or ***chiyl***. This information is useful because the study of root words can often give a fuller understanding of the word being studied.

❑ Circle or highlight the word history listing.

> **H2428** חַיִל *hayil* from H2342; probably a *force,* whether of men, means or other resources; an *army, wealth, virtue, valor, strength:*— able, activity, army, army, band of men, band of soldiers, company, forces, great forces, goods, host, might, power, riches, strength, strong, substance, train, valiant, valiant, valiantly, valour, virtuous, virtuously, war, worthy, worthily.

D. Next the **concise meaning** of the word is listed. This portion ends with a colon(:)

❏ Circle or highlight this portion

> **H2428** חַיִל *hayil* from H2342; probably a *force,* whether of men, means or other resources; an *army, wealth, virtue, valor, strength:*— able, activity, army, army, band of men, band of soldiers, company, forces, great forces, goods, host, might, power, riches, strength, strong, substance, train, valiant, valiant, valiantly, valour, virtuous, virtuously, war, worthy, worthily.

E. Following the meaning, the colon, and the dash mark (:—), are all the different English renderings of the original Hebrew word. These are the different words that the translators of the King James Version chose to use when translating this particular Hebrew word into English. For this Hebrew word, the translators used more than twenty different English words!

❏ Circle or highlight this portion

> **H2428** חַיִל *hayil* from H2342; probably a *force,* whether of men, means or other resources; an *army, wealth, virtue, valor, strength:*— able, activity, army, army, band of men, band of soldiers, company, forces, great forces, goods, host, might, power, riches, strength, strong, substance, train, valiant, valiant, valiantly, valour, virtuous, virtuously, war, worthy, worthily.

Day 3 - Studying the word "valour"

A. Open to a blank page in your notebook and write "Valour" at the top of the page. Copy all the references that are listed under "valour" in Strong's (put one reference on each line and leave room to write notes by each one).

Look up and read each of the references you listed, and take notes on what each verse says about valour or men of valour.

Day 4 - Summarize

Read over your notes and summarize what you learned:

A. Which men in the Bible are called men of valor?

_____

_____

_____

_____

_____

_____

_____

_____

B. What actions do men of valor do?

_____

_____

_____

_____

_____

_____

_____

C. What is a man of valor?

_____

_____

_____

_____

_____

_____

Day 5 - Find other uses of the Hebrew word:

A. We have now read all the verses that contained the Hebrew word "*hayil*" when it was translated as "valour." To continue our study, we will return to the definition of the word as we found it in the Hebrew word dictionary.

In order to study more passages in the Bible that contain this same Hebrew word, *hayil*, we will look at some other English renderings of the word as they are translated in the King James Version. These words are all listed after the dash (—).

B. List these words:

_____

_____

_____

_____

_____

_____

_____

More than twenty English words are used to represent the word *hayil*, but we will focus on the words that are most relevant to our study.

(Note: to quickly read ALL the verses using the word *hayil*, use Blue Letter Bible [as outlined on p.38] or E-Sword [instructions on the left] to pull up a list of all verses in the Bible that use this Hebrew word. This will be much faster and easier than looking up all the different words in the concordance.)

C. Go back to the concordance and look up the word **valiant**.

How many of the verses listed under **valiant** use the Hebrew word 2428?

_____

D. Label another page in your notebook **valiant**. Read the verses that use 2428 *hayil* and note what you learn in your notebook.

E. Find the word **valiantly** (probably on the same page). How many of these verses use the Hebrew word 2428? _____ Read these verses and note what you learn in your notebook.

Day 6 - Other words

A. The word 2428 is sometimes translated **might**. Since this is also a common word with a different meaning, it is harder to find the verses that use the word **hayil**.

Look up 2 Kgs. 24:16, 1 Chr. 7:2, Ps. 76:5, and Zec. 4:6 and note what is said about **might** in your notebook.

B. Next look up the word **virtuous** in the concordance, read any verses that use the word 2428, and take notes in your notebook.

C. The word **virtuously** right below it also lists one verse that uses our word 2428. Look up this verse and take notes in your notebook.

D. Repeat this process for the words **power**, **strength**, and **wealth**, taking notes in your notebook. You're almost done!

Day 7 - Summarize

Review all the notes you made as you read verses using the word ***hayil***, and answer the following questions:

A. What characterizes men of valor? What does it mean to be a man of valor?

_____

_____

_____

_____

_____

_____

_____

_____

_____

_____

_____

Englishman's Concordances

To quickly find verses that use a specific Hebrew or Greek word without using computer study tools (see previous page), use the reference books **Englishman's Hebrew and Chaldee Concordance** or **Englishman's Greek Concordance**.

B. ✳ What does a man of valor do?

_____

_____

_____

_____

_____

_____

_____

_____

_____

_____

C. Where can we find strength to be men of valor?

_____

_____

_____

D. What do you admire about men of valor in the Bible?

_____

_____

_____

_____

_____

_____

E. What else did you learn?

_____

_____

_____

_____

_____

F. ✱ Do you know any men who fit the biblical definition of "men of valor" today? Who are they?

_____

_____

_____

_____

_____

_____

_____

_____

Day 8 - Application:

A. ✱ How can you become more of a man of valor?

_____

_____

_____

_____

_____

_____

_____

_____

B. Pray for the Holy Spirit to help you see how God wants you to change. Write down **a specific goal** for application in your own life. Ask someone to hold you accountable!

_____

_____

_____

_____

_____

_____

_____

_____

_____

_____

_____

For additional study:

- The word "valiant" is used one time in the New Testament, in Heb. 11:34. The Greek word translated "valiant" here is the same word that's translated "strong" in 1 John 2:14 ("I have written unto you, young men, because ye are *strong*"). Conduct a New Testament word study on this Greek word, using the same methods you just used in this study.

- Another synonym of strength in the Old Testament is the word "power." Use the word study methods from this study to find the original Hebrew word and its definition, and study other verses that use this word.

- In the phrase "mighty man of valor," the Hebrew word for "mighty" is "gibbor". Use the same word study methods from this study to study the Hebrew word "gibbor". How is it different from "hayil"?

- The word for valor is sometimes used in reference to "able men," or "men of activity". Conduct a topical study on "diligence" using Strong's Concordance and the topical study method from Study 3.

Strength in Our Weakness

A Verse Study on 2 Corinthians 12:9-10

"But he said to me, 'My grace is sufficient for you, for my power is made perfect in weakness.'
Therefore I will boast all the more gladly of my weaknesses, so that the power of Christ may rest upon me.
For the sake of Christ, then, I am content with weaknesses, insults, hardships, persecutions, and calamities.
For when I am weak, then I am strong." (2 Corinthians 12:9-10, ESV)

We see God work mightily through unlikely people and circumstances over and over again in Scripture. Gideon saved Israel from the Midianite hordes with a band of 300. David killed a giant with just a sling and a stone. Jesus, the Son of God, made His earthly appearance as a baby born in a stable, and He won the battle against sin and death by dying a criminal's death on a cross.

Our weaknesses and hardships are an opportunity for God's power to be displayed. When we face trials, we need to hold fast to God and rely on His strength instead of our own.

In this study, we'll focus on studying a particular verse (actually two verses in this study). We can gain greater insight into a verse or passage by reading the context, and by using the marginal notes found in many Bibles.

Day 1 - Read verses and paraphrase

A. Read and copy 2 Corinthians 12:9-10 in two different Bible translations below. Reading in different translations helps you understand a verse better and see how different translators interpreted it.

_____

_____

_____

_____

_____

_____

_____

_____

Verse study (focus on cross-references):

1. Read the verse in several translations.

2. Write your own paraphrase.

3. Read the context.

4. Write down any observations and lessons from the verse.

5. Use marginal notes to find cross-references, read, and note observations.

6. Summary and application

What you will need:

- At least two Bibles in different translations

- A Bible with marginal notes

_____

_____

_____

_____

You can use an online parallel Bible to compare different
translations of a verse or
passage (see p. 77).

_____

_____

_____

_____

_____

_____

_____

_____

_____

B. Now, write a paraphrase of 2 Corinthians 12:9-10. Try to convey the
same meaning, but in your own words.

_____

_____

_____

_____

_____

_____

_____

_____

_____

_____

_____

_____

_____

_____

Day 2 - Context

In order to understand the verses we're studying, we need to read the chapters and verses before and after them. We need to know what the writer is talking about. Considering the context is very important when studying verses and short passages of Scripture.

A. Read 2 Corinthians 10-12 to better understand the context of these verses.

B. What problem is Paul addressing in these chapters? (11:1-15, 12:11-12)

_____

_____

_____

_____

C. What else do you learn from 2 Corinthians 10-12?

_____

_____

_____

_____

_____

_____

D. Write down any questions you have about this passage or its context:

_____

_____

_____

_____

> **Interpreting Scripture with Scripture**
>
> "The infallible rule of interpretation of scripture is the scripture itself; and therefore, when there is a question about the true and full sense of any scripture, it must be searched and known by other places that speak more clearly."
>
> *The Westminster Confession of Faith, 1646*

Day 3 - Using Marginal Notes

Now we are going to dig deeper into the meaning of 2 Corinthians 12:9-10 by using the marginal notes found in your Bible. You will see that these notes are very helpful!

Many styles of marginal notes exist. You might need to look through the beginning pages of your Bible and find the section that explains its particular cross-referencing system.

A. Look carefully at 2 Corinthians 12:9-10 in your Bible. Besides the obvious text of the verses and the verse numbers, do you see any other small numbers or letters in the verses? Some Bibles also have a column of small words along one margin or between the columns of Scripture text.

If you don't see these numbers, letters, or small text, examine other Bibles in your home until you find one with marginal references. Most study Bibles should have the marginal references we need for this study. If you can see examples in an actual Bible, the explanation offered here will be easier to understand.

Most Bibles with marginal references mark words and phrases within the verse with "superscript" numbers and letters. "Superscript" means that the letters and numbers are **smaller** and **raised higher** than the rest of the type in the text.

In the page's reference column (found in the margin, or in between columns of Scripture text), bold numbers will indicate verse numbers, and after each verse number will appear any notes pertaining to that particular verse.

Textual notes are additional information that the Bible translators wanted us to know about. Often these notes will shed light on the meaning of a word or give possible alternate readings of a verse. In some cases, these notes also indicate sections that are different from one ancient manuscript to another. Textual notes are most often indicated with superscript numbers.

> **8** *Matt. 26:44*
>
> **9** *Later mss. read My power*
> *1 Cor. 2:5; Eph. 3:16; Phil. 4:13*
> *1 Cor. 2:3; 2 Cor. 12:5*
>
> **10** *Or, mistreatment*
> *Rom. 5:3; 8:35*
> *2 Cor. 6:4*
> *2 Thess. 1:4; 2 Tim. 3:11*
> *2 Cor. 5:15, 20*
> *2 Cor. 13:4*

> 9 And He has said to me, "My grace is sufficient for you, for *1a*power is perfected in weakness." Most gladly, therefore, I will rather *b*boast about my weaknesses, that the power of Christ may dwell in me.
> 10 (Therefore) *a*I am well content with weaknesses, with *1*insults, with *b*distresses, with *c*persecutions, with *b*difficulties, *d*for Christ's sake; for *e*when I am weak, then I am strong.
> 11 I have become *a*foolish; you yourselves compelled me. Actually I should have been commended by you, for *b*in no respect was I inferior to the *1*most eminent apostles, even though *c*I am a nobody.
> 12 The *1a*signs *2*of a true apostle were performed among you with all perseverance, by *1*signs and wonders and *3*miracles.
> 13 For in what respect were you treated as inferior to the rest of the

For example, in the **New International Inductive Study Bible**, there is a superscript "1" before the word "power" in 2 Corinthians 12:9. In the marginal notes, we find a bold number **9**, indicating these notes are relevant to verse 9. In the notes next to this **9**, we look for the small "1". This is where we find a textual note: "1 Later mss read *My power.*" This means that in some Greek manuscripts, the text reads "my power," while in others, it simply reads "power." This helps clarify what already appears likely—that the verse is talking primarily about God's power being manifested through Paul's weakness.

As another example, in the **New Inductive Study Bible**, there is a superscript "1" before the word "insults" in 2 Corinthians 12:10. We look in the marginal notes for verse 10, then find the small "1". This is where we find a textual note: "1 Or, mistreatment". This means that the translators of this Bible version wanted us to know that the word "insults" could also be translated "mistreatment".

Common types of marginal notes:

- **Textual notes** give information related to the translation and original languages. These notes may tell you about other possible translations of a word or about small differences in the text of the original manuscripts.

- **Cross-references** point you to other Bible verses that are related to the ones you are reading.

- **Other notes** often explain unfamiliar terms and units of measure.

B. In your study Bible, look for any marginal notes on 2 Corinthians 12:9-10 that contain textual information. Note anything you find here:

_____

_____

_____

_____

_____

Day 4 - Cross References

The other, and most common type of marginal notes are **cross references**. These are references to other verses that relate to or shed light on the verses you are reading.

A. In the **New Inductive Study Bible**, there is a superscript "ᵃ" before the word "power" in 2 Corinthians 12:9. We look in the marginal notes for verse 9, then find the small "ᵃ". This is where we find the cross references :

> ᵃ 1 Cor. 2:5; Eph. 3:16; Phil. 4:13

These verses relate to the phrase "…power is perfected in weakness" in 2 Corinthians 12:9.

B. Look up each of these verses, and note what they say. How are they related to 2 Corinthians 12:9?

1 Corinthians 2:5

_____

_____

_____

Ephesians 3:16

_____

_____

_____

Philippians 4:13

_____

_____

_____

A note about notes:

It is important to remember that marginal notes are not the divinely inspired Word of God. They are editors' notes, written by scholars who have studied the Bible and its original languages. These notes are not infallible. They are influenced by the editors' theology and by different understandings of languages and words.

Find Cross References with Blue Letter Bible

1. Search for "1 Cor 12:9" at www.blueletterbible.org.

2. If using the website, hover over "tools" button for the verse and then select "Cross-Refs".

3. If using the app, tap the verse and then "Cross-References (TSK)".

4. You will see the text of the verse with certain words highlighted. Scroll down to read other Bible verses that share a similar theme or shed more light on different parts of the verse you are studying.

Using marginal references at Biblegateway.com.

1. Go to www.biblegateway.com and look up 2 Corinthians 12:9-10 in the verse search box.

2. This should bring up the text of the verse. Above this text, you should see a button for "page options".

3. Click the "page options" button, and you should see a list of checkboxes for "footnotes," "cross references," etc. Check these buttons to show the marginal notes. Links for each cross reference will be displayed below the verse text.

C. 2 Corinthians 12:9 also has a superscript "b" before the word "boast". The references listed under the small "b" in the margin are 1 Corinthians 2:3 and 2 Corinthians 12:5. Read these verses. What do they say? How do they relate to 2 Corinthians 12:9?

1 Corinthians 2:3

_____

_____

_____

2 Corinthians 12:5

_____

_____

_____

Day 5 - More cross-references

A. The **ESV Study Bible** lists two additional cross-references for 2 Corinthians 12:9. Read Isaiah 43:2 and Isaiah 40:29-31. What do these verses say? How do they relate to 2 Corinthians 12:9?

Isaiah 43:2

_____

_____

_____

_____

_____

Isaiah 40:29-31

_____

_____

_____

_____

_____

_____

_____

B. In your reference Bible, look at 2 Corinthians 12:10. Do you see any superscript letters? Find any cross-references and list them here. Look up each of these verses, and record what you learn.

Reference: Notes:

_____

_____

_____

_____

_____

_____

_____

_____

_____

_____

_____

_____

C. Here are some more cross references for this passage, collected from different study Bibles. Check off any references that you already read in step B above, and then look up the remaining references. Summarize what you learn from each verse:

Deuteronomy 8:2-3 _____

_____

Psalm 84:11 _____

_____

Romans 8:35-36 _____

_____

Matthew 5:11-12 _____

_____

1 Corinthians 1:25-31 _____

_____

2 Corinthians 1:3-6 _____

_____

2 Corinthians 4:7 _____

_____

2 Corinthians 5:20-21 _____

_____

2 Corinthians 6:3-6 _____

_____

2 Corinthians 8:9 _____

_____

2 Corinthians 9:8 _____

_____

2 Corinthians 13:4 _____

_____

Ephesians 2:8 _____

_____

Philippians 4:19 _____

_____

2 Thessalonians 1:3-4 _____

_____

2 Timothy 3:10-11 _____

_____

2 Timothy 4:6-8 _____

_____

Day 6 - Insights/Lessons:

Review what you have written about 2 Corinthians 12:9-10 and the other verses you read in this study, and answer the following questions:

A. For what reasons does God allow us to suffer or experience weakness?

_____

_____

_____

_____

_____

_____

_____

_____

_____

_____

_____

_____

_____

B. We find strength by…

_____

_____

_____

_____

_____

_____

_____

_____

_____

_____

C. What else did you learn from this study?

_____

_____

_____

_____

_____

_____

_____

_____

_____

_____

Day 7 - Application

A. How do the lessons of this study apply to you? Pray that God will show you, by His Holy Spirit, what He wants you to learn from His Word. In what areas do you need to change? Do you have the right attitude towards trials and suffering? What effect do trials have on you? How is the power of Christ evident in your life? Take time to think about this. Review your notes from the study. Pray for God's help.

_____

_____

_____

_____

_____

_____

_____

_____

_____

_____

B. Commit now to applying what you've learned. List at least one specific thing you will do in obedience to God's Word over the next week. Be very specific. Focus primarily on things you will **do**, not only what you will **stop** doing. Ask your parents to pray for you and hold you accountable. Review your goals next week with one of your parents.

_____

_____

_____

_____

_____

_____

_____

_____

_____

_____

_____

_____

For additional study:

- You can gain additional insight into a verse or passage by studying the key words in the passage. We'll do this in Study 9. Use the word study methods in Study 9 to look up the key words from 2 Corinthians 12:9-10.

- Do a topical study on afflictions. Follow the topical study method from Study 2, and look up "Afflictions" and "Suffering" in Nave's Topical Bible.

- Job was a man who was faithful to God in the midst of severe trials. Conduct either a book study of the book of Job (see Study 10) or a character study of Job (see Study 4).

- Study 1 Peter 4:10-11 using the same methods you used in this study.

Strength in the Battle

A Chapter Study of 1 Samuel 17

"For the battle is the LORD's, and he will give you into our hand." (1 Samuel 17:47b)

1 Samuel 17 tells of a dramatic face-off between an arrogant giant-warrior with armor and huge weapons, and a young boy with only a sling and some little rocks. The outcome proved that true strength isn't determined by size, ability, or experience, but by what's in your heart.

In this study, we will analyze one chapter of Scripture and look for structure, repeated themes, and central lessons. We'll also look up cross references and consult a Bible commentary to gain further insight.

Day 1 - Read the chapter and context

A. Read 1 Samuel 17, along with chapters 15-19 to get the context for this story.

Day 2 - Outline

A. Read 1 Sam. 17 again and outline the main events of the chapter:

v. 1-11 _____

v. 12-23 _____

v. 24-30 _____

v. 31-37 _____

v. 38-40 _____

v. 41-47 _____

v. 48-51 _____

v. 52-58 _____

Chapter study

1. Read the chapter and context.

2. Outline the chapter, note main people and events.

3. Look for key words and themes.

4. Check for cross-references.

5. Consult Bible commentaries.

6. Central lessons

7. Application

What you will need:

• Bibles in two different translations, at least one with marginal notes

• Matthew Henry's commentary

Day 3 - People

Look for the main people mentioned in this chapter. (You may want to color each name a different color in your Bible.) Read the whole chapter again and note what is said about each person:

A. Saul _____

_____

_____

_____

B. Goliath _____

_____

_____

_____

_____

_____

C. David _____

_____

_____

_____

_____

_____

_____

_____

_____

_____

D. Jesse _____

_____

_____

E. Eliab _____

_____

_____

Day 4 - Key words and themes

A. Read the chapter again, and select one verse that best encapsulates the theme or point of the chapter. Copy this verse here:

_____

_____

_____

_____

_____

B. List at least two key words that are significant or repeated in this chapter:

_____

_____

Day 5 - Read cross references

A. If your Bible doesn't have cross references, find a study Bible that does. List each reference below, along with the verse it's listed by. (You may or may not use all the spaces, depending on what Bible you have.) Now look up each verse and summarize what it says or how it relates to the chapter we are studying.

You can also find cross references using online Bibles (see p. 52 and 53).

Verse: Cross Ref.   Verse summary:

_____ _____ _____

_____ _____ _____

_____ _____ _____

_____ _____ _____

_____ _____ _____

_____ _____ _____

_____ _____ _____

Verse: Cross Ref.   Verse summary:

_____   _____   _____

_____   _____   _____

_____   _____   _____

_____   _____   _____

_____   _____   _____

_____   _____   _____

_____   _____   _____

Online commentaries

• Matthew Henry's com-
mentary, and several
others, are online at www.
biblestudytools.com. Go to
their site and click on the
"commentaries" tab. You
can also get the entire set
of Matthew Henry's com-
mentaries for about $5.00
for the Amazon Kindle.

• In Blue Letter Bible, tap
the verse or hover on the
"tools" button and then
select "commentaries".
You'll find a whole list of
commentaries and even
audio messages related to
the verse you are studying.

• Free Bible commentaries
can also be downloaded
with e-Sword and other
mobile apps (see page 7).

Day 6 - Using a Bible commentary:

A good Bible commentary can often help you answer questions that you
have as you are studying the Bible. It will also be a helpful resource if you
have your own family some day. Notes from a commentary can help you
prepare lessons for family worship or answer questions that your wife or
children ask.

For this study, we will use **Matthew Henry's Commentary on the
Whole Bible**. Though it was written three hundred years ago, this com-
mentary is readily available, very practical, and often used by pastors and
Bible teachers today.

A. Read 1 Samuel 17 again, noting any questions you have or things that
are unclear to you:

_____

_____

_____

_____

B. Look up 1 Samuel 17 in Matthew Henry's Commentary on the Whole
Bible. (You will need **Volume II**, which covers Joshua to Esther, unless
you have a one-volume edition. The entire commentary is also available
online for free.)

Read Matthew Henry's commentary for this chapter and answer the questions below. Look for answers to the questions you wrote down earlier.

C. What does the commentary say about David and his character? What prepared him to fight Goliath? What gave him his confidence?

_____

_____

_____

_____

_____

_____

D. What does the commentary say about Saul and his character? Why do you think he didn't fight Goliath?

_____

_____

E. The commentary points out several contrasts between David and Goliath in this story. List any that you notice from reading the Scripture text or the commentary:

David: Goliath:

_____   _____

_____   _____

_____   _____

_____   _____

_____   _____

F. Did you find answers to any of your questions? Write any answers here:

_____

_____

_____

_____

Matthew Henry's Commentary

Matthew Henry was a Presbyterian minister who lived from 1662 to 1714. His father Phillip gathered his family every day for morning and evening devotions, where he would read a Scripture passage, explain it, and encourage the children to write their own notes. Although he was often in poor health, Matthew had an aptitude for study, and it is said that he could read the Bible by age three. (He also learned Latin, Greek, and Hebrew.)

At age twenty-three, he went to London to study law, but he found it unsatisfying and returned home after only one year. It was then that a friend asked him to preach, and he discovered the work God had designed him for. So great was his enthusiasm for the gospel, and so thorough was his preparation for each sermon, that other churches soon began asking him to come and preach.

Before long, he was offered a pastorate in the town of Chester, and he served there as a pastor for over twenty-five years. Toward the end of his life, he gathered his many notes from Bible study and preaching and wrote a commentary on the entire Old Testament, along with the Gospels and the book of Acts. Sadly, he died before his commentary on the New Testament was finished. Henry's pastor friends realized the value of his practical, easily understandable commentary, and they used his notes on Romans through Revelation to complete the project and produce the Bible commentary that has been widely used ever since.

Day 7 - Central lessons

A. Look for Christ pictured. Since all of God's Word is meant to point us to Jesus, we can learn about Him, or at least see Him pictured, in almost any chapter of the Bible. Read 1 Samuel 17 again and note any ways that you see Christ in this chapter:

What similarities do you notice between David and Jesus?

_____

_____

_____

_____

B. Central lessons. Read the chapter one more time. Look for the central lessons, the message of this chapter. Also consider the cross-references you looked up. What can you learn from this chapter?

_____

_____

_____

_____

_____

_____

_____

Day 8 - Conclusion and Application

A. Re-read what you just wrote down about lessons you've learned from 1 Samuel 17. How do these lessons apply to your own life? How can you be more like David?

_____

_____

_____

_____

_____

_____

_____

_____

_____

_____

_____

_____

For further study:

B. What are you going to do about it? List at least two things you will do to apply the lessons you've learned. Set goals that are specific and measurable:

_____

_____

_____

_____

_____

_____

_____

_____

_____

_____

- Do a study on "zeal" using the topical study method from Study 2. Look up "zeal" in Nave's Topical Bible, and read the verses under "Exemplified," and "Instances of," and take notes. Who in the Bible was zealous? What were they zealous for? What did they do as a result of their zeal?

- Conduct a character study of David, following the character study method outlined in Study 4.

- Study the life of Saul, and compare the lives of David and Saul. How was each man strong? How was each man weak?

- Use the verse study method from Study 6 to study Ephesians 6:11-20 and learn about the Armor of God.

Study 8

Strength Serving Others

A Study of Jesus' Actions
in the Gospel of Mark

*"For even the Son of man came not to be ministered unto, but to minister,
and to give his life a ransom for many." (Mark 10:45)*

There is much we can learn from Jesus' life. Being the good teacher that
He is, he taught many things by example. While we can learn much from
His words, we can also learn much from His actions. Though He was
all-powerful, He used His power to serve, not to force others to serve him.
Pray that the Holy Spirit will work through God's Word to help you truly
see Jesus and learn from His life.

A thorough character study on Jesus would take a long time, since so
much of the Bible is written about him. We will narrow the scope of our
study by focusing on a specific aspect of Jesus' character, His *actions*, and
by limiting our study to the gospel of Mark.

Day 1-4 - Read and mark

A. Read through the gospel of Mark. Watch carefully for any time that
Jesus' actions are mentioned, and mark each action with a colored pencil
or highlighter. You'll get through all 16 chapters in four days if you read
four chapters each day.

Day 5 - Review what you marked

Once you have marked the verses that talk about Jesus' actions, it will
be easy to skim over the verses you marked and answer the following
questions:

A. What are the most common actions you see Jesus doing?

_____

_____

_____

_____

_____

_____

Character + topical study

1. Choose the topic or person you want to study.

2. Read a chapter, book, or several books of the Bible, marking sections relevant to your topic or character.

3. Analyze and summarize your observations.

4. Application

What you will need:

- A Bible you can mark in

- One colored pencil or highlighter

B. How does Jesus resist evil and temptation?

_____

_____

_____

_____

_____

Day 6 - Review what you marked

A. What makes Jesus angry?

_____

_____

_____

_____

_____

B. How does Jesus show kindness to others?

_____

_____

_____

_____

_____

_____

_____

Day 7 - Review what you marked

A. How does Jesus stay focused on His mission?

_____

_____

_____

_____

_____

B. How is Jesus a good leader to His disciples?

_____

_____

_____

_____

_____

Day 8 - Review what you marked

A. What makes Jesus a good teacher?

_____

_____

_____

_____

_____

B. How is Jesus' power demonstrated? Does He exercise His power for His own benefit, or for the benefit of others?

_____

_____

_____

_____

_____

Day 9 - Application

A. Review your answers above. Note anything that Jesus does that you can imitate:

_____

_____

_____

_____

_____

_____

Keep your study notes on the computer:

Keeping your study notes in a text document on your computer has several advantages:

- It's _easier to save your notes_ in case you want to review them or share them with someone else.

- It can help you _organize notes_ and _analyze your findings_ without having to re-write your notes over and over.

- It also allows you e_asily save verses and excerpts from your reference materials_—simply copy these and paste them into your study notes.

On the other hand, a computer can be a distraction to Bible study if you have email or other programs running at the same time.

You can use a word processor like Microsoft Word, Notepad, Pages, or Google Drive to type notes for your Bible study. Read straight through the book of Mark, taking notes about any of Jesus' actions. It will be easy to go back over these notes when you're done and organize them using "cut & paste". Just create headings for each of the questions below, then cut anything that relates to that question from your notes and paste it under that heading.

_____

_____

_____

_____

_____

_____

B. Pray that God would show you how you can be more like Jesus. In what ways is God calling you to change after studying the example of Jesus?

_____

_____

_____

_____

_____

_____

_____

For further study:

- Study Philippians 2:5-8 using the verse study methods in Study 6.

- Study Romans 15:1-3 using the verse study methods in Study 6.

- Moses spent much of his life serving others. Use the character study method from Study 4 and conduct a character study of Moses.

- Conduct a topical study on the purpose of Jesus' ministry. Look up "Jesus, the Christ – Mission of" in Nave's Topical Bible and use the topical study methods from Study 2.

C. Choose two specific ways that you can imitate Jesus with your actions today. Then do them!

_____

_____

_____

_____

_____

_____

_____

_____

_____

_____

Strength and Gray Heads

A Verse Study of Proverbs 20:29

"The glory of young men is their strength: and the beauty of old men is the gray head."
(Proverbs 20:29)

This Proverb compares the strength of young men and the gray head of old men, saying that both are worthy of honor. Studying this verse will give us a better perspective on the seasons of life and help us make good use of our God-given abilities.

Our first verse study (Study 6) focused on using marginal notes, but in this study, we will examine the main words in Proverbs 20:29, seeking to gain a better understanding of the verse's meaning. Like many Proverbs, this verse seems simple, but when you dig in, there is a lot to chew on!

Day 1 - Studying the words

You learned how to look up Hebrew words in Strong's Concordance in Study 5. We will again use Strong's to study each of the six key words in this verse. Knowing the Hebrew definitions and usage will help us understand this verse better.

"The glory of young men is their strength: and the beauty of old men is the gray head." (Proverbs 20:29)

A. Look up the word **glory** in Strong's (see below). Scan the list of references until you find Prov. 20:29, then look at the number in the right hand column of that listing. This is the dictionary number that tells you where to find the original Hebrew word in the dictionary section of Strong's.

Prv	3:35 The wise shall inherit **g**: but shame	H3519
	4: 9 a crown of **g** shall she deliver to thee.	H8597
	16:31 The hoary head *is* a crown of **g**, *if* it be	H8597
	17: 6 and the **g** of children *are* their fathers.	H8597
	19:11 *it is* his **g** to pass over a transgression.	H8597
	20:29 The **g** of young men *is* their strength:	H8597
	25: 2 *It is* the **g** of God to conceal a thing: but	H3519
	27 *men* to search their own **g** *is not* glory.	H3519

What is the Strong's number for the word **glory** in Prov. 20:29? _____

Now turn to the Hebrew dictionary section of Strong's (remember, it's after the concordance and before the Greek dictionary). Look up this number and find the original word and its definition.

What is the Hebrew word for glory in Prov. 20:29? _____

Verse study (focus on original words):

1. Study important words in the verse.

2. Write your own paraphrase.

3. Read in several translations.

4. Read the context and any cross-references.

5. Ask questions and meditate on the verse

6. Application

What you will need:

• At least two Bibles in different translations

• A Bible with cross references

• Strong's Concordance

You can also look up these words in Strong's Concordance online (see p. 21)

What is the definition of this word? _____

_____

After the definition, Strong's lists other ways this word was translated in the KJV Bible. Looking at these other English words will give you more insight into the meaning of the word. What other English words are listed?

_____

_____

_____

_____

You can also use a "Strong's Number Search" to quickly look up these verses and others that use the same Hebrew word (see page 42).

Who was denied **honor** because he lacked confidence in God's plan?

(Judg. 4:8-9) _____

When is a hoary head a crown of **glory**? (Prov. 16:31) _____

_____

B. Look up the word **beauty** in Strong's. Scan the list of references until you find Prov. 20:29, then look at the number in the right hand column of that listing. What is the Strong's dictionary number for the word **beauty** in Prov. 20:29? _____

Look up this number in the Hebrew dictionary of Strong's and find the original word and its definition.

What is the Hebrew word for **beauty** in Prov. 20:29? _____

What is the definition of this word? _____

_____

What other English words are used to translate this Hebrew word?

_____

_____

_____

What is full of **majesty**? (Psalm 29:4) _____

_____

Strength and **honour** are whose clothing? (Prov. 31:25) _____

_____

Whose **beauty** has departed? (Lam. 1:6) _____

Day 2 - More words

A. The two words "young men" in this verse are actually translated from one Hebrew word. Look up the word **young** in Strong's to find it. Scan the list of references until you find Prov. 20:29, then look at the number in the right hand column of that listing. What is the Strong's dictionary number for the word **young** in Prov. 20:29? _____

Look up this number in the Hebrew dictionary of Strong's and find the original word and its definition.

What is the Hebrew word for **young men** in Prov. 20:29? _____

What is the definition of this word? _____

_____

What other English words are used to translate this Hebrew word?

_____

_____

_____

_____

Who could have followed **young men**, but didn't? (Ruth 3:10)

_____

Why did David gather all the **chosen men** of Israel? (2 Sam. 6:1-2)

_____

What should a **young man** do in his youth? (Eccl. 11:9-10)

_____

Who will renew their strength even when the **young men** "utterly fall"? (Isa. 40:30-31)

_____

B. The two words "old men" in this verse are actually translated from one Hebrew word. Look up the word **old** in Strong's to find it. Scan the list of references until you find Prov. 20:29, then look at the number in the right hand column of that listing. What is the Strong's dictionary number for the word **old** in Prov. 20:29? _____

Look up this number in the Hebrew dictionary of Strong's and find the original word and its definition.

What is the Hebrew word for **old men** in Prov. 20:29? _____

Interlinear Bibles online

An interlinear Bible displays the verse you are studying along with the text in the original Greek or Hebrew. You can look up Proverbs 20:29 in an interlinear Bible online and quickly find all the original words and their definitions.

Blue Letter Bible

1. Go to www.blueletterbible.com (or use the mobile app).

2. Search for "Prov 20:29".

3. On the website, hover over "tools" and select "interlinear". In the app, tap the verse and then select "interlinear/concordance".

4. You'll see the verse broken down into words and short phrases, each with its corresponding Hebrew word and Strong's number. If you click the Strong's number it will take you to a wealth of study info about that word, including a definition and all the other verses in the Bible that use the same word.

Bible Study Tools

1. Go to www.biblestudytools.com.

2. Under the "Read" tab, click "Interlinear Bible".

3. Search for "Prov 20:29".

4. You will see the verse in English on top, and the verse in the original Hebrew below. Many of the words in this text are links.

5. Click any of the linked words to view the original word, the definition, and a list of other places that word is used in the Bible.

What is the definition of this word? _____

_____

What other English words are used to translate this Hebrew word?

_____

_____

_____

Look up and read the following verses that use this word:

What job were the **elders** of Israel given in this passage? (Num. 11:11-17)

_____

How should you treat **old men**? (Lev. 19:32)

_____

Who gave the wisest advice? The **old men,** or the young men? (1 Kgs. 12:1-16)

_____

In what way can even an **old** king act foolishly? (Eccl. 4:13)

_____

_____

What made David wiser than the **ancients**? (Psalm 119:100)

_____

What is the crown of **old men**? (Prov. 17:6)

_____

Day 3 - More words

A. Look up the word **strength** in Strong's. Scan the list of references until you find Prov. 20:29, then look at the number in the right hand column of that listing. What is the Strong's dictionary number for the word **strength** in Prov. 20:29? _____

Look up this number in the Hebrew dictionary of Strong's and find the original word and its definition.

What is the Hebrew word for **strength** in Prov. 20:29? _____

What is the definition of this word? _____

_____

What other English words are used to translate this Hebrew word?

_____

_____

_____

Look up and read the following verses that use this word:

How did Jacob serve Laban? (Gen. 31:6) _____

_____

Through whom did God show His **power**? (Ex. 9:16) _____

Who was still **strong** at age 85? (Josh. 14:10-11) _____

How can you avoid wasting your labor and filling strangers with your **wealth**? (Prov. 5:3-10)

_____   _____

What comes by the **strength** of the ox? (Prov. 14:4) _____

Who was punished by God for proudly claiming **strength** as his own? (Isa. 10:12-13)

_____

B. The two words "gray head" in this verse are actually translated from one Hebrew word. Look up the word **gray** in Strong's to find it. Scan the list of references until you find Prov. 20:29, then look at the number in the right hand column of that listing. What is the Strong's dictionary number for the word **gray** in Prov. 20:29? _____

Look up this number in the Hebrew dictionary of Strong's and find the original word and its definition.

What is the Hebrew word for **gray head** in Prov. 20:29? _____

What is the definition of this word? _____

_____

What other English phrases are used to translate this Hebrew word?

_____

_____

_____

_____

Look up and read the following verses that use this word:

Who died at a good **old age?**

Genesis 25:8 _____

Judges 8:32 _____

1 Chronicles 29:26-28 _____

Who still brings forth fruit in **old age**? (Ps. 92:12-15) _____

The **hoary head** is a crown of glory, if... (Prov. 16:31)

_____

_____

What does the psalmist want to do, even when he is old and **grayheaded**? (Ps. 71:18)

_____

_____

_____

Compare Bible translations with an online parallel Bible

Online study tools like Blue Letter Bible can help you quickly compare different Bible translations of a verse. This will help you see how different scholars translated the original Hebrew or Greek words into English. This will give us a better understanding of the key words in this verse.

1. Go to www.blueletterbible.com.

2. Search for "Prov 20:29".

3. On the web, click "Tools" and then "Bibles". In the app, tap the verse, then tap "Translation Comparison".

4. You'll see the verse in a *bunch* of different Bible translations. The BLB website even lets you

Based on your study of these words, write a paraphrase of Proverbs 20:29 in your own words:

_____

_____

_____

_____

Read Proverbs 20:29 in two or three different Bible translations to see how the words you studied are translated differently in other Bibles.

Day 4 - Context and cross references

In the average verse study, the context is very important. Ignoring the context of a verse can often cause serious misunderstandings. The context in Proverbs is less important, though, because most of the proverbs stand on their own. Still, Proverbs does have structure and themes, and you may find some related wisdom if you read the surrounding verses.

A. Read the context of this verse (chapters 20-21 of Proverbs). Do any verses in these chapters seem related to this verse? Do you spot any similar words, topics, or themes? Copy any verses that seem related:

_____

_____

_____

_____

_____

_____

_____

_____

_____

_____

_____

B. Look up any cross references for Proverbs 20:29. If your Bible does not have cross references in the margin, find a study Bible with cross references. These are usually listed in a separate column to one side of the Bible text, or at the bottom of each page (see study 6).

You can also look up cross references in an online Bible (see p. 52 or p. 53)..

What cross reference(s) do you find for Proverbs 20:29?

_____

_____

C. What do these verse(s) say that relates to the verse you are studying?

_____

_____

_____

_____

D. ✻ Read Titus 2:1-8. What does Paul tell Titus to teach the younger men?

_____

_____

_____

E. ✻ What instructions for older men are given in Titus 2:2?

_____

_____

_____

Day 5 - Questions and meditation

Remember the six questions we used in Study 1? Use use these questions again as you meditate on Proverbs 20:29:

A. WHO is this verse comparing to one another?

_____

_____

The six questions:

- Who?
- What?
- Why?
- When?
- Where?
- How?

B. WHAT qualities are being compared? Are they the same? If not, what is the difference between the two?

_____

_____

_____

_____

_____

C. WHERE do we see the truth of this verse played out?

_____

_____

D. WHEN does this apply to us? When we are young men, what can we learn? What can we learn if we are in the older, wiser season of life?

_____

_____

_____

_____

_____

E. WHY is a young man's strength beautiful? Why might young men be proud of their strength? What would make a young man's strength more beautiful or less beautiful? Why is gray hair majestic? Why do we show honor to elders? Why should we? Why doesn't God give us maximum strength and wisdom at the same time in our life?

_____

_____

_____

_____

_____

_____

_____

_____

_____

_____

_____

_____

F. HOW are young men strong? How is gray hair beautiful? How do old men become wise? Are all old men wise?

_____

_____

_____

_____

_____

_____

Day 6 - Another way to think about this verse

A. Draw your own chart, or complete the graph below showing the relationship in a person's life of age, strength, and wisdom. Draw one line graphing your *expected strength* over the course of your life. Then draw another showing your *expected wisdom* (with the bottom of the chart being no strength/wisdom and the top being lots of strength/wisdom).

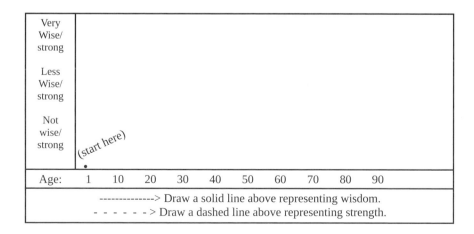

B. What can you learn from this graph you just drew?

_____

_____

_____

C. When do you expect your greatest physical strength?

_____

D. When do you expect to be wisest?

_____

E. Do your lines cross anywhere? Do you ever expect the two qualities to be equal?

_____

_____

_____

F. How can young men compensate for their lack of wisdom?

_____

_____

_____

G. How can old men compensate for their lessened strength?

_____

_____

_____

Day 7 - Application

Now, consider what you've learned from this verse and how it applies to your life.

A. ✳ How old are you? Are you a young man or an old man? What implications for people your age have we uncovered?

_____

_____

_____

_____

_____

_____

_____

B. ✱ If you are a young man, name five specific older people you can show honor to:

_____

_____

_____

_____

_____

C. How, specifically, can you show honor to each of the five people you listed above?

_____

_____

_____

_____

_____

D. Who are five specific godly, older men or women who you would turn to for counsel?

_____

_____

_____

_____

_____

E. Are you in the position of "elder" to anyone now? Who?

_____

_____

For further study:

• Draw another graph like the one on p.79. Make this one larger, and draw the same lines showing your expected strength and wisdom near the middle. Now, pick a different colored pen and draw two more sets of lines, one starting before yours, and one starting after. These will represent your parents and your children (you can add your grandparents too, if you want. Make sure every line has the same shape as yours, but offset each by 25-30 years in either direction. Can you see how one generation's wisdom and another's strength overlap? Why do you think God made it that way?

• Look up Proverbs 20:29 in two or more Bible commentaries and take notes (see p. 62).

• Using the same methods from this study, study Isaiah 40:29-31.

• Using the verse study methods from Study 6, study Exodus 20:12 and look for ways to honor your parents and other authorities in your life.

F. How can you share wisdom or be a good example to those younger than you?

G. What can you do now to pursue wisdom so that you will grow wiser as you get older?

Strength in the Faith

A Book Study of 1 John

"I write to you, young men, because you are strong, and the word of God abides in you, and you have overcome the evil one." (1 John 2:14b, ESV)

The epistle of 1 John was written to help early Christians avoid being deceived and drawn away from the true faith. In studying this book, we'll discover many directions for staying strong in our faith and overcoming the evil one.

The book of 1 John is packed with meaning and application, and a pastor could spend years preaching through it. The purpose of this study is to get an overview of 1 John as a whole book, and to look specifically at what 1 John says about strengthening our faith. The steps in this study can be applied to any other book of the Bible you want to study.

Day 1 - Pray & read

A. Begin your study with prayer. Read all five chapters of 1 John, preferably in one sitting.

Day 2 - Read again

A. Read 1 John a second time in a different translation. This helps you think about the text and understand it better.

Day 3 - Background information

Get some background information on the book. Refer to a study bible or commentary to answer the following questions:

A. Who wrote the book of 1 John?

_____

_____

_____

B. Approximately what time was the book written?

_____

_____

Book study:

1. Read the book several times through.

2. Look up background info for the book in a study Bible or commentary.

3. Look for and mark specific themes in the book.

4. Summarize each chapter and create an outline.

5. Answer additional questions and summarize lessons you find in the book.

6. Application

What you will need:

- Two Bibles in different translations

- A study Bible or Bible dictionary

- Matthew Henry's commentary

C. Where was it written?

_____

_____

_____

D. Who was it written for?

_____

_____

_____

E. Why was it written?

_____

_____

_____

F. What is the key message or purpose of this book?

_____

_____

_____

G. What historical events preceded the writing of 1 John?

_____

_____

_____

H. What historical events came shortly after the writing of 1 John?

_____

_____

_____

I. Where does this book fit in the Bible? Is it a transition between different periods of history?

_____

_____

_____

J. What other background information sheds light on this book?

_____

_____

_____

_____

_____

_____

Day 4 - 1 John at a glance

Read a third time, and look for answers to these questions:

A. What is the purpose of the book?

_____

B. What are some key words you see repeated through the book?

_____

_____

_____

C. What are the main themes you see in this book?

_____

_____

_____

Literary styles in the Bible :
• Law
• History
• Wisdom Literature
• Poetry
• Prophecy
• Gospel
• Epistles

D. What is the style of the book?

_____

E. Do you see any major divisions or sections within the book of 1 John?

_____

F. Are there major characters in this book? Who are they?

_____

Listen to sermon audio from the web

Some pastors, like John Piper, have been making their sermons available online for decades, and many churches now offer downloadable recordings of their sermons. You can listen online from your computer, or save the audio recording to an MP3 player and listen to it in the car, while you work, or when you exercise.

Visit one of the following sites and listen to a sermon on 1 John:

- www.sermonaudio.com
- www.desiringGod.org
- www.wordMP3.com (some free, some paid)
- Your church's website
- Websites by other pastors or Bible teachers you respect
- In Blue Letter Bible (website and app), you can find sermons and audio related to any passage in the "tools" section under "commentaries".

G. Choose one or two key verses and copy them. Pick a passage that you think sums up the overall message of 1 John.

_____

_____

_____

_____

_____

_____

_____

Day 5 - Outline the book

One part of a book study is identifying the structure and flow of the book you are studying. The structure of 1 John is not as clear as most books of the Bible, but there are still themes that you can identify. Keep in mind that chapter and verse numbers in our Bibles were not part of the original, inspired writing of the Scriptures, and these chapter divisions don't always align with the logical structure of the book.

Read a fourth time and assign a title to each chapter:

Chapter 1: _____

Chapter 2: _____

Chapter 3: _____

Chapter 4: _____

Chapter 5: _____

Look for any major divisions in the book and make your own outline of 1 John:

_____

_____

_____

_____

_____

_____

_____

_____

_____

_____

_____

_____

_____

_____

Day 6 - Key passage, consulting a commentary

Now we will dig deeper and look at the key messages and themes in 1 John.

1 John 2:12-14 is an important passage to examine as we study godly strength. Read these verses again.

A. Why does John write to the "children"?

_____

_____

_____

_____

B. Why does John write to the "fathers"?

_____

_____

_____

_____

C. Why does John write to the "young men"?

_____

_____

_____

_____

We can get additional insights on these verses by consulting a Bible commentary. Look up 1 John 2:12-14 in Matthew Henry's Commentary and read the commentary for these verses.

For more about Matthew Henry's Commentary, see p. 62-63

D. Who does Matthew Henry think the "children" are in this passage? What is distinct about this group of people?

_____

_____

_____

_____

E. Who does Matthew Henry think the "fathers" are in this passage? What is distinct about this group of people?

_____

_____

_____

_____

F. Who does Matthew Henry think the "young men" are in this passage? What is distinct about this group of people?

_____

_____

_____

_____

G. What supplies "young men" with strength and enables them to overcome the evil one?

_____

_____

_____

Day 7 - Key words

Several topics are repeated throughout the book. We're going to look for six of these key topics by marking some specific words, then taking notes. You can do this slowly in one pass, marking all the words, or take several quicker passes through the book looking for one word at a time. Colors are suggested for each word; feel free to use your own marking system.

A. Skim the book and mark the word "**world**" with a distinct color (orange).

Read back over each time this word is used, and note what is said about the **world**:

_____

_____

_____

_____

_____

_____

_____

_____

_____

_____

_____

_____

B. Skim the book and mark the word "**abide**" with a distinct color (brown).

Read back over each time this word is used, and note what is said about **abiding**:

_____

_____

_____

_____

_____

_____

_____

_____

_____

_____

_____

_____

_____

_____

_____

_____

C. Skim the book and mark the words "**life**," "**live**," and "**eternal life**" in a distinct way (yellow).

Read back over each time these words are used, and note what is said about **life**:

_____

_____

_____

_____

_____

_____

_____

_____

_____

_____

_____

Day 8 - More key words

A. Skim the book and mark the words "**children**" or "**little children**" with a distinct color (green).

Read back over each time these words are used, and note what is said to or about **children**:

_____

_____

_____

_____

_____

_____

_____

_____

_____

_____

_____

_____

B. Skim the book and mark the word "**evil one**," "**darkness**," and "**devil**" with a distinct color (red).

Read back over each time these words are used, and note what is said:

_____

_____

_____

_____

_____

_____

_____

_____

C. Skim the book and mark the word "**overcome**," and any related terms, with a distinct color (blue).

Read back over each time this word is used, and note what is said about **overcoming**:

_____

_____

_____

_____

_____

_____

_____

Day 9 - Finding answers to questions

A. Note any questions you have after reading and studying 1 John:

_____

_____

_____

_____

_____

For notes on using online commentaries, see p. 62.

B. Talk with your parents or pastor, or consult a commentary to find answers to these questions. Write down any answers that you find:

_____

_____

_____

_____

_____

_____

_____

_____

Day 10 - Summary

1 John says a lot about how Christians should live, and why we should live this way. Review your study notes so far, and read 1 John one more time, looking for answers to the following questions:

A. Why can/should you be strong in your faith?

_____

_____

_____

_____

_____

_____

B. What should give you confidence?

_____

_____

_____

_____

_____

_____

C. What helps you overcome evil?

_____

_____

_____

_____

_____

_____

D. What should the life of a strong believer look like?

_____

_____

_____

_____

_____

_____

_____

_____

_____

_____

_____

_____

_____

E. Summarize your findings. Describe how 1 John calls you to act and think as a Christian.

_____

_____

_____

_____

_____

_____

_____

_____

_____

_____

_____

_____

_____

_____

_____

Day 11 - Application

Pray for the Holy Spirit to show you what God wants you to learn from your study. Then write out a specific application.

A. How is God calling you to change? What can make you stronger in your faith? Does the word of God "abide in you"? In what areas of your life do you need to "overcome the evil one"?

_____

_____

_____

_____

_____

B. Copy a verse from 1 John that you will memorize.

_____

_____

_____

_____

_____

_____

_____

For further study:

- Listen to one or more sermons on 1 John from the Internet.

- Look up 1 John 2:12-14 in several commentaries and note your findings.

- Study the book of Nehemiah, using the same methods you used in this study. Pay special attention to the character of Nehemiah, how he shows strength as a leader, and what motivates him to be strong.

- Write an essay entitled "How to be strong in the faith" based on what you learned in this study.

- Choose a verse from 1 John to study in more detail. Use the verse study methods from Study 6 or Study 9.

Strength in Review

God's Word shows us what true strength looks like and gives us lots of good examples we can look to. In this study, you've seen godly strength from many different angles. You've also used quite a few different Bible study methods by now. Take a few more days to review what you've learned.

Day 1 - What is biblical strength?

Write an essay on strength from a biblical perspective, considering the following questions:

- Where can we find godly examples of strength?

- What is the source of true strength?

- What should motivate Christians to be strong?

- Why does God give us strength? How should our strength be spent?

- Why is self-control important?

- Why is wisdom important?

- What things can overcome physical strength?

_____

_____

_____

_____

_____

_____

_____

_____

_____

_____

_____

_____

_____

Day 2 - A truly strong man

✱ Think of a strong Christian man that you know. Observe him, consider his life, and record your observations.

How does he respond to God's Word?

_____

_____

How does he interact with other people?

_____

_____

How does he serve others?

_____

_____

How does he treat his wife?

_____

_____

How does he treat his children?

_____

_____

How does he treat others under his authority?

_____

_____

How does he treat those in authority over him?

_____

_____

How does he use his God-given talents?

_____

_____

How does he use his time?

_____

_____

How does he respond to trials and difficulties in his life?

_____

_____

Day 3 - Areas to grow in

How can you grow in godly strength? Pray again for God's guidance.

Are there specific areas in your life that you know, with the Holy Spirit's help, need to change? Get some advice from a parent or a wiser, older man, and outline a specific plan to help you grow in godly strength. Then follow the plan!

_____

_____

_____

_____

_____

_____

_____

_____

_____

Day 4 - Types of Bible study

Explain how to perform a topical study in the Bible. How do you find out more about a specific topic in the Bible? What study tools will help you? (See Studies 2 and 3).

_____

_____

_____

_____

Explain how to study a Bible character. How can you find all the passages that tell about a specific person in the Bible? What kind of details should you look for as you read about the person? (See Study 4)

_____

_____

_____

_____

Explain how to study a book of the Bible. What different steps will help you better understand the book? How can you find background information on a book of the Bible? (See Study 10)

_____

_____

_____

_____

What six questions will help you meditate on a verse or passage of Scripture? (See Study 1)

_____

What study tool can help you find the original Hebrew or Greek words used in a Bible passage? How do you find the definition of that word? How do you find other verses that use the same word? (See Study 5)

_____

_____

_____

What helpful information is provided in a Bible's marginal notes? (see Study 6)

_____

_____

Future study topics. At this point, and over time, you may think of other words, topics, passages, and people that you would like to study more. Use this area to record other studies you would like to pursue in the future. After you finish a study, you can refer to this list to find ideas for your next study.

_____

_____

_____

_____

Alternate Questions for Young Ladies

Study 3, Day 5 A

✻ Based on what you have just learned, what can you do to be a stronger woman or to use your strength more wisely? Look specifically at the example of the virtuous woman in Proverbs 31. Is there a specific area where God is calling you to exercise your strength or to grow stronger in?

_____

_____

_____

_____

Study 4, Day 3 F

✻ Women had a powerful influence on Samson. When they pressed, he gave in. In the story of Samson, we twice see women overcome his great strength through deception. Throughout the Bible, we see women use deception in ungodly and also in godly ways. God worked mightily through godly women who deceived the enemies of God. Read about these women and note how God used their deception to accomplish His purposes and overpower evil men:

Jael. (Judges 4:17-22)

_____

_____

Rahab. (Joshua 2:1-21)

_____

_____

Esther. (Esther 2:20, 5:1-8, 7:1-6)

_____

_____

Michal. (1 Samuel 19:11-17)

_____

_____

Study 5, Day 7 B

✻ Which women in the Bible demonstrate *valor*? What do they do?

_____

_____

_____

_____

Study 5, Day 7 F

✻ Do you know any women who fit the biblical definition of "valiant" or "virtuous" today? Who are they?

_____

_____

_____

_____

_____

Study 5 day 8 A

✻ How can you become a more virtuous woman?

_____

_____

_____

_____

_____

_____

Study 9, day 4 D

✻ Read Titus 2:1-8. What does Paul say the older women should teach the younger women?

_____

_____

_____

_____

Study 9, day 4 E

✻ What instructions for older women are given in Titus 2:3?

_____

_____

_____

_____

✲ How old are you? Are you a young woman or an older one? What implications for people your age have we uncovered?

Study 9, Day 7 A

_____

_____

_____

_____

_____

✲ If you are a young woman, name five specific older people you can show honor to:

Study 9, Day 7 B

_____

_____

_____

_____

_____

✲ Think of a strong Christian woman that you know. Observe her, consider her life, and record your observations.

Strength in Review, Day 2

How does she respond to God's Word?

_____

_____

How does she interact with other people?

_____

_____

How does she serve others?

_____

_____

How does she treat her husband?

_____

_____

How does she treat her children?

_____

_____

How does she use her God-given talents?

_____

_____

How does she use her time?

_____

_____

How does she respond to trials and difficulties in her life?

_____

_____

Beauty in the Heart contains ten Bible studies on godly beauty for young ladies, in a similar style to this book. Visit www.doorposts.com for more details.